THIS LOG BOO[K]

NAME: _____

ADDRESS: _____

_____

PHONE NUMBER: _____

LOG BOOK DETAILS:

LOG START DATE: _____

LOG END DATE: _____

LOGBOOK NUMBER: _____

HUNTING JOURNAL AND LOG BOOK

GAME BEING PERSUED _____

DATE: _____ TIME: _____ TO: _____

WEATHER DETAILS
CURRENT TEMP: _____ HIGH/LOW: _____ / _____
MOON PHASE: _____ BAROMETER: _____
SUNRISE: _____ SUNSET: _____

ELEMENTS
WIND DIRECTION: _____ SPEED: _____

CIRCLE ONE: SUNNY - PARTLY CLOUDY - CLOUDY - RAINING - STORMING

PREHUNT PREP
BAIT: _____ STAND/BLIND: _____
SCENT: _____ CALL USED: _____
DECOY: _____

RESULTS: _____
_____

ANIMAL ACTIVITY
SIGHTINGS (CIRCLE)
FEEDING - DROPPINGS - TRACKS - SCRAPES/RUBS
OTHER: _____
NUMBER OF ANIMALS SEEN / SEX: _____

HARVEST NOTES
WEAPON USED: _____ ANIMAL SIZE: _____

OTHER FIELD NOTES: _____
_____
_____
_____
_____

HUNTING JOURNAL AND LOG BOOK

GAME BEING PERSUED _____

DATE: _____ TIME: _____ TO: _____

WEATHER DETAILS
CURRENT TEMP: _____ HIGH/LOW: _____ / _____
MOON PHASE: _____ BAROMETER: _____
SUNRISE: _____ SUNSET: _____

ELEMENTS
WIND DIRECTION: _____ SPEED: _____

CIRCLE ONE: SUNNY – PARTLY CLOUDY – CLOUDY – RAINING – STORMING

PREHUNT PREP
BAIT: _____ STAND/BLIND: _____
SCENT: _____ CALL USED: _____
DECOY: _____
RESULTS: _____
_____

ANIMAL ACTIVITY
SIGHTINGS (CIRCLE)
FEEDING – DROPPINGS – TRACKS – SCRAPES/RUBS
OTHER: _____
NUMBER OF ANIMALS SEEN / SEX: _____

HARVEST NOTES
WEAPON USED: _____ ANIMAL SIZE: _____

OTHER FIELD NOTES: _____
_____
_____
_____
_____

HUNTING JOURNAL AND LOG BOOK

GAME BEING PERSUED _____

DATE: _____ TIME: _____ TO: _____

WEATHER DETAILS

CURRENT TEMP: _____ HIGH/LOW: _____ / _____

MOON PHASE: _____ BAROMETER: _____

SUNRISE: _____ SUNSET: _____

ELEMENTS

WIND DIRECTION: _____ SPEED: _____

CIRCLE ONE: SUNNY - PARTLY CLOUDY - CLOUDY - RAINING - STORMING

PREHUNT PREP

BAIT: _____ STAND/BLIND: _____

SCENT: _____ CALL USED: _____

DECOY: _____

RESULTS: _____

_____

ANIMAL ACTIVITY

SIGHTINGS (CIRCLE)

FEEDING - DROPPINGS - TRACKS - SCRAPES/RUBS

OTHER: _____

NUMBER OF ANIMALS SEEN / SEX: _____

HARVEST NOTES

WEAPON USED: _____ ANIMAL SIZE: _____

OTHER FIELD NOTES: _____

_____

_____

_____

_____

HUNTING JOURNAL AND LOG BOOK

GAME BEING PERSUED _____

DATE: _____ TIME: _____ TO: _____

WEATHER DETAILS
CURRENT TEMP: _____ HIGH/LOW: _____ / _____
MOON PHASE: _____ BAROMETER: _____
SUNRISE: _____ SUNSET: _____

ELEMENTS
WIND DIRECTION: _____ SPEED: _____
CIRCLE ONE: SUNNY – PARTLY CLOUDY – CLOUDY – RAINING – STORMING

PREHUNT PREP
BAIT: _____ STAND/BLIND: _____
SCENT: _____ CALL USED: _____
DECOY: _____
RESULTS: _____
_____

ANIMAL ACTIVITY
SIGHTINGS (CIRCLE)
FEEDING – DROPPINGS – TRACKS – SCRAPES/RUBS
OTHER: _____
NUMBER OF ANIMALS SEEN / SEX: _____

HARVEST NOTES
WEAPON USED: _____ ANIMAL SIZE: _____

OTHER FIELD NOTES: _____
_____
_____
_____
_____

HUNTING JOURNAL AND LOG BOOK

GAME BEING PERSUED _____

DATE: _____ TIME: _____ TO: _____

WEATHER DETAILS
CURRENT TEMP: _____ HIGH/LOW: _____ / _____
MOON PHASE: _____ BAROMETER: _____
SUNRISE: _____ SUNSET: _____

ELEMENTS
WIND DIRECTION: _____ SPEED: _____

CIRCLE ONE: SUNNY – PARTLY CLOUDY – CLOUDY – RAINING – STORMING

PREHUNT PREP
BAIT: _____ STAND/BLIND: _____
SCENT: _____ CALL USED: _____
DECOY: _____
RESULTS: _____
_____

ANIMAL ACTIVITY
SIGHTINGS (CIRCLE)
FEEDING – DROPPINGS – TRACKS – SCRAPES/RUBS
OTHER: _____
NUMBER OF ANIMALS SEEN / SEX: _____

HARVEST NOTES
WEAPON USED: _____ ANIMAL SIZE: _____

OTHER FIELD NOTES: _____
_____
_____
_____
_____
_____

HUNTING JOURNAL AND LOG BOOK

GAME BEING PERSUED _____

DATE: _____ TIME: _____ TO: _____

WEATHER DETAILS
CURRENT TEMP: _____ HIGH/LOW: _____ / _____
MOON PHASE: _____ BAROMETER: _____
SUNRISE: _____ SUNSET: _____

ELEMENTS
WIND DIRECTION: _____ SPEED: _____

CIRCLE ONE: SUNNY – PARTLY CLOUDY – CLOUDY – RAINING – STORMING

PREHUNT PREP
BAIT: _____ STAND/BLIND: _____
SCENT: _____ CALL USED: _____
DECOY: _____
RESULTS: _____
_____

ANIMAL ACTIVITY
SIGHTINGS (CIRCLE)
FEEDING – DROPPINGS – TRACKS – SCRAPES/RUBS
OTHER: _____
NUMBER OF ANIMALS SEEN / SEX: _____

HARVEST NOTES
WEAPON USED: _____ ANIMAL SIZE: _____

OTHER FIELD NOTES: _____
_____
_____
_____
_____

HUNTING JOURNAL AND LOG BOOK

GAME BEING PERSUED _____

DATE: _____ TIME: _____ TO: _____

WEATHER DETAILS
CURRENT TEMP: _____ HIGH/LOW: _____ / _____
MOON PHASE: _____ BAROMETER: _____
SUNRISE: _____ SUNSET: _____

ELEMENTS
WIND DIRECTION: _____ SPEED: _____

CIRCLE ONE: SUNNY - PARTLY CLOUDY - CLOUDY - RAINING - STORMING

PREHUNT PREP
BAIT: _____ STAND/BLIND: _____
SCENT: _____ CALL USED: _____
DECOY: _____
RESULTS: _____
_____

ANIMAL ACTIVITY
SIGHTINGS (CIRCLE)
FEEDING - DROPPINGS - TRACKS - SCRAPES/RUBS
OTHER: _____
NUMBER OF ANIMALS SEEN / SEX: _____

HARVEST NOTES
WEAPON USED: _____ ANIMAL SIZE: _____

OTHER FIELD NOTES: _____
_____
_____
_____
_____

HUNTING JOURNAL AND LOG BOOK

GAME BEING PERSUED _____

DATE: _____ TIME: _____ TO: _____

WEATHER DETAILS
CURRENT TEMP: _____ HIGH/LOW: _____ / _____
MOON PHASE: _____ BAROMETER: _____
SUNRISE: _____ SUNSET: _____

ELEMENTS
WIND DIRECTION: _____ SPEED: _____
CIRCLE ONE: SUNNY – PARTLY CLOUDY – CLOUDY – RAINING – STORMING

PREHUNT PREP
BAIT: _____ STAND/BLIND: _____
SCENT: _____ CALL USED: _____
DECOY: _____
RESULTS: _____
_____

ANIMAL ACTIVITY
SIGHTINGS (CIRCLE)
FEEDING – DROPPINGS – TRACKS – SCRAPES/RUBS
OTHER: _____
NUMBER OF ANIMALS SEEN / SEX: _____

HARVEST NOTES
WEAPON USED: _____ ANIMAL SIZE: _____

OTHER FIELD NOTES: _____
_____
_____
_____
_____

HUNTING JOURNAL AND LOG BOOK

GAME BEING PERSUED _____

DATE: _____ TIME: _____ TO: _____

WEATHER DETAILS
CURRENT TEMP: _____ HIGH/LOW: _____ / _____
MOON PHASE: _____ BAROMETER: _____
SUNRISE: _____ SUNSET: _____

ELEMENTS
WIND DIRECTION: _____ SPEED: _____
CIRCLE ONE: SUNNY – PARTLY CLOUDY – CLOUDY – RAINING – STORMING

PREHUNT PREP
BAIT: _____ STAND/BLIND: _____
SCENT: _____ CALL USED: _____
DECOY: _____
RESULTS: _____
_____

ANIMAL ACTIVITY
SIGHTINGS (CIRCLE)
FEEDING – DROPPINGS – TRACKS – SCRAPES/RUBS
OTHER: _____
NUMBER OF ANIMALS SEEN / SEX: _____

HARVEST NOTES
WEAPON USED: _____ ANIMAL SIZE: _____

OTHER FIELD NOTES: _____
_____
_____
_____
_____

HUNTING JOURNAL AND LOG BOOK

GAME BEING PERSUED _____

DATE: _____ TIME: _____ TO: _____

WEATHER DETAILS
CURRENT TEMP: _____ HIGH/LOW: _____ / _____
MOON PHASE: _____ BAROMETER: _____
SUNRISE: _____ SUNSET: _____

ELEMENTS
WIND DIRECTION: _____ SPEED: _____

CIRCLE ONE: SUNNY - PARTLY CLOUDY - CLOUDY - RAINING - STORMING

PREHUNT PREP
BAIT: _____ STAND/BLIND: _____
SCENT: _____ CALL USED: _____
DECOY: _____
RESULTS: _____
_____

ANIMAL ACTIVITY
SIGHTINGS (CIRCLE)
FEEDING - DROPPINGS - TRACKS - SCRAPES/RUBS
OTHER: _____
NUMBER OF ANIMALS SEEN / SEX: _____

HARVEST NOTES
WEAPON USED: _____ ANIMAL SIZE: _____

OTHER FIELD NOTES: _____
_____
_____
_____
_____

HUNTING JOURNAL AND LOG BOOK

GAME BEING PERSUED _____

DATE: _____   TIME: _____   TO: _____

WEATHER DETAILS
CURRENT TEMP: _____   HIGH/LOW: _____ / _____
MOON PHASE: _____   BAROMETER: _____
SUNRISE: _____   SUNSET: _____

ELEMENTS
WIND DIRECTION: _____   SPEED: _____
CIRCLE ONE: SUNNY – PARTLY CLOUDY – CLOUDY – RAINING – STORMING

PREHUNT PREP
BAIT: _____   STAND/BLIND: _____
SCENT: _____   CALL USED: _____
DECOY: _____
RESULTS: _____
_____

ANIMAL ACTIVITY
SIGHTINGS (CIRCLE)
FEEDING – DROPPINGS – TRACKS – SCRAPES/RUBS
OTHER: _____
NUMBER OF ANIMALS SEEN / SEX: _____

HARVEST NOTES
WEAPON USED: _____ ANIMAL SIZE: _____

OTHER FIELD NOTES: _____
_____
_____
_____
_____

HUNTING JOURNAL AND LOG BOOK

GAME BEING PERSUED _____

DATE: _____   TIME: _____   TO: _____

WEATHER DETAILS

CURRENT TEMP: _____   HIGH/LOW: _____/_____

MOON PHASE: _____   BAROMETER: _____

SUNRISE: _____   SUNSET: _____

ELEMENTS

WIND DIRECTION: _____   SPEED: _____

CIRCLE ONE: SUNNY - PARTLY CLOUDY - CLOUDY - RAINING - STORMING

PREHUNT PREP

BAIT: _____   STAND/BLIND: _____

SCENT: _____   CALL USED: _____

DECOY: _____

RESULTS: _____

_____

ANIMAL ACTIVITY

SIGHTINGS (CIRCLE)
FEEDING - DROPPINGS - TRACKS - SCRAPES/RUBS

OTHER: _____

NUMBER OF ANIMALS SEEN / SEX: _____

HARVEST NOTES

WEAPON USED: _____   ANIMAL SIZE: _____

OTHER FIELD NOTES: _____

_____

_____

_____

_____

HUNTING JOURNAL AND LOG BOOK

GAME BEING PERSUED _____

DATE: _____   TIME: _____   TO: _____

WEATHER DETAILS
CURRENT TEMP: _____   HIGH/LOW: _____ / _____
MOON PHASE: _____   BAROMETER: _____
SUNRISE: _____   SUNSET: _____

ELEMENTS
WIND DIRECTION: _____   SPEED: _____
CIRCLE ONE: SUNNY - PARTLY CLOUDY - CLOUDY - RAINING - STORMING

PREHUNT PREP
BAIT: _____   STAND/BLIND: _____
SCENT: _____   CALL USED: _____
DECOY: _____
RESULTS: _____
_____

ANIMAL ACTIVITY
SIGHTINGS (CIRCLE)
FEEDING - DROPPINGS - TRACKS - SCRAPES/RUBS
OTHER: _____
NUMBER OF ANIMALS SEEN / SEX: _____

HARVEST NOTES
WEAPON USED: _____   ANIMAL SIZE: _____

OTHER FIELD NOTES: _____
_____
_____
_____
_____

HUNTING JOURNAL AND LOG BOOK

GAME BEING PERSUED _____

DATE: _____ TIME: _____ TO: _____

WEATHER DETAILS
CURRENT TEMP: _____ HIGH/LOW: _____ / _____
MOON PHASE: _____ BAROMETER: _____
SUNRISE: _____ SUNSET: _____

ELEMENTS
WIND DIRECTION: _____ SPEED: _____

CIRCLE ONE: SUNNY – PARTLY CLOUDY – CLOUDY – RAINING – STORMING

PREHUNT PREP
BAIT: _____ STAND/BLIND: _____
SCENT: _____ CALL USED: _____
DECOY: _____
RESULTS: _____
_____

ANIMAL ACTIVITY
SIGHTINGS (CIRCLE)
FEEDING – DROPPINGS – TRACKS – SCRAPES/RUBS
OTHER: _____
NUMBER OF ANIMALS SEEN / SEX: _____

HARVEST NOTES
WEAPON USED: _____ ANIMAL SIZE: _____

OTHER FIELD NOTES: _____
_____
_____
_____
_____

HUNTING JOURNAL AND LOG BOOK

GAME BEING PERSUED _____

DATE: _____ TIME: _____ TO: _____

WEATHER DETAILS
CURRENT TEMP: _____ HIGH/LOW: _____ / _____
MOON PHASE: _____ BAROMETER: _____
SUNRISE: _____ SUNSET: _____

ELEMENTS
WIND DIRECTION: _____ SPEED: _____

CIRCLE ONE: SUNNY – PARTLY CLOUDY – CLOUDY – RAINING – STORMING

PREHUNT PREP
BAIT: _____ STAND/BLIND: _____
SCENT: _____ CALL USED: _____
DECOY: _____
RESULTS: _____
_____

ANIMAL ACTIVITY
SIGHTINGS (CIRCLE)
FEEDING – DROPPINGS – TRACKS – SCRAPES/RUBS
OTHER: _____
NUMBER OF ANIMALS SEEN / SEX: _____

HARVEST NOTES
WEAPON USED: _____ ANIMAL SIZE: _____

OTHER FIELD NOTES: _____
_____
_____
_____
_____

HUNTING JOURNAL AND LOG BOOK

GAME BEING PERSUED _____

DATE: _____ TIME: _____ TO: _____

WEATHER DETAILS
CURRENT TEMP: _____ HIGH/LOW: _____ / _____
MOON PHASE: _____ BAROMETER: _____
SUNRISE: _____ SUNSET: _____

ELEMENTS
WIND DIRECTION: _____ SPEED: _____

CIRCLE ONE: SUNNY – PARTLY CLOUDY – CLOUDY – RAINING – STORMING

PREHUNT PREP
BAIT: _____ STAND/BLIND: _____
SCENT: _____ CALL USED: _____
DECOY: _____
RESULTS: _____
_____

ANIMAL ACTIVITY
SIGHTINGS (CIRCLE)
FEEDING – DROPPINGS – TRACKS – SCRAPES/RUBS
OTHER: _____
NUMBER OF ANIMALS SEEN / SEX: _____

HARVEST NOTES
WEAPON USED: _____ ANIMAL SIZE: _____

OTHER FIELD NOTES: _____
_____
_____
_____
_____

HUNTING JOURNAL AND LOG BOOK

GAME BEING PERSUED _____

DATE: _____ TIME: _____ TO: _____

WEATHER DETAILS
CURRENT TEMP: _____ HIGH/LOW: _____ / _____
MOON PHASE: _____ BAROMETER: _____
SUNRISE: _____ SUNSET: _____

ELEMENTS
WIND DIRECTION: _____ SPEED: _____

CIRCLE ONE: SUNNY – PARTLY CLOUDY – CLOUDY – RAINING – STORMING

PREHUNT PREP
BAIT: _____ STAND/BLIND: _____
SCENT: _____ CALL USED: _____
DECOY: _____
RESULTS: _____
_____

ANIMAL ACTIVITY
SIGHTINGS (CIRCLE)
FEEDING – DROPPINGS – TRACKS – SCRAPES/RUBS
OTHER: _____
NUMBER OF ANIMALS SEEN / SEX: _____

HARVEST NOTES
WEAPON USED: _____ ANIMAL SIZE: _____

OTHER FIELD NOTES: _____
_____
_____
_____
_____

HUNTING JOURNAL AND LOG BOOK

GAME BEING PERSUED _____

DATE: _____ TIME: _____ TO: _____

WEATHER DETAILS
CURRENT TEMP: _____ HIGH/LOW: _____ / _____
MOON PHASE: _____ BAROMETER: _____
SUNRISE: _____ SUNSET: _____

ELEMENTS
WIND DIRECTION: _____ SPEED: _____

CIRCLE ONE: SUNNY - PARTLY CLOUDY - CLOUDY - RAINING - STORMING

PREHUNT PREP
BAIT: _____ STAND/BLIND: _____
SCENT: _____ CALL USED: _____
DECOY: _____
RESULTS: _____
_____

ANIMAL ACTIVITY
SIGHTINGS (CIRCLE)
FEEDING - DROPPINGS - TRACKS - SCRAPES/RUBS
OTHER: _____
NUMBER OF ANIMALS SEEN / SEX: _____

HARVEST NOTES
WEAPON USED: _____ ANIMAL SIZE: _____

OTHER FIELD NOTES: _____
_____
_____
_____
_____

HUNTING JOURNAL AND LOG BOOK

GAME BEING PERSUED _____

DATE: _____ TIME: _____ TO: _____

WEATHER DETAILS
CURRENT TEMP: _____ HIGH/LOW: _____ / _____
MOON PHASE: _____ BAROMETER: _____
SUNRISE: _____ SUNSET: _____

ELEMENTS
WIND DIRECTION: _____ SPEED: _____
CIRCLE ONE: SUNNY - PARTLY CLOUDY - CLOUDY - RAINING - STORMING

PREHUNT PREP
BAIT: _____ STAND/BLIND: _____
SCENT: _____ CALL USED: _____
DECOY: _____
RESULTS: _____
_____

ANIMAL ACTIVITY
SIGHTINGS (CIRCLE)
FEEDING - DROPPINGS - TRACKS - SCRAPES/RUBS
OTHER: _____
NUMBER OF ANIMALS SEEN / SEX: _____

HARVEST NOTES
WEAPON USED: _____ ANIMAL SIZE: _____

OTHER FIELD NOTES: _____
_____
_____
_____
_____

HUNTING JOURNAL AND LOG BOOK

GAME BEING PERSUED _____

DATE: _____   TIME: _____   TO: _____

WEATHER DETAILS
CURRENT TEMP: _____   HIGH/LOW: _____ / _____
MOON PHASE: _____   BAROMETER: _____
SUNRISE: _____   SUNSET: _____

ELEMENTS
WIND DIRECTION: _____   SPEED: _____

CIRCLE ONE: SUNNY - PARTLY CLOUDY - CLOUDY - RAINING - STORMING

PREHUNT PREP
BAIT: _____   STAND/BLIND: _____
SCENT: _____   CALL USED: _____
DECOY: _____
RESULTS: _____
_____

ANIMAL ACTIVITY
SIGHTINGS (CIRCLE)
FEEDING - DROPPINGS - TRACKS - SCRAPES/RUBS
OTHER: _____
NUMBER OF ANIMALS SEEN / SEX: _____

HARVEST NOTES
WEAPON USED: _____   ANIMAL SIZE: _____

OTHER FIELD NOTES: _____
_____
_____
_____
_____

HUNTING JOURNAL AND LOG BOOK

GAME BEING PERSUED _____

DATE: _____ TIME: _____ TO: _____

WEATHER DETAILS
CURRENT TEMP: _____ HIGH/LOW: _____ / _____
MOON PHASE: _____ BAROMETER: _____
SUNRISE: _____ SUNSET: _____

ELEMENTS
WIND DIRECTION: _____ SPEED: _____

CIRCLE ONE: SUNNY – PARTLY CLOUDY – CLOUDY – RAINING – STORMING

PREHUNT PREP
BAIT: _____ STAND/BLIND: _____
SCENT: _____ CALL USED: _____
DECOY: _____
RESULTS: _____
_____

ANIMAL ACTIVITY
SIGHTINGS (CIRCLE)
FEEDING – DROPPINGS – TRACKS – SCRAPES/RUBS
OTHER: _____
NUMBER OF ANIMALS SEEN / SEX: _____

HARVEST NOTES
WEAPON USED: _____ ANIMAL SIZE: _____

OTHER FIELD NOTES: _____
_____
_____
_____
_____

HUNTING JOURNAL AND LOG BOOK

GAME BEING PERSUED _____

DATE: _____ TIME: _____ TO: _____

WEATHER DETAILS
CURRENT TEMP: _____ HIGH/LOW: _____ / _____
MOON PHASE: _____ BAROMETER: _____
SUNRISE: _____ SUNSET: _____

ELEMENTS
WIND DIRECTION: _____ SPEED: _____

CIRCLE ONE: SUNNY – PARTLY CLOUDY – CLOUDY – RAINING – STORMING

PREHUNT PREP
BAIT: _____ STAND/BLIND: _____
SCENT: _____ CALL USED: _____
DECOY: _____
RESULTS: _____
_____

ANIMAL ACTIVITY
SIGHTINGS (CIRCLE)
FEEDING – DROPPINGS – TRACKS – SCRAPES/RUBS
OTHER: _____
NUMBER OF ANIMALS SEEN / SEX: _____

HARVEST NOTES
WEAPON USED: _____ ANIMAL SIZE: _____

OTHER FIELD NOTES: _____
_____
_____
_____
_____

HUNTING JOURNAL AND LOG BOOK

GAME BEING PERSUED _____

DATE: _____ TIME: _____ TO: _____

WEATHER DETAILS
CURRENT TEMP: _____ HIGH/LOW: _____ / _____
MOON PHASE: _____ BAROMETER: _____
SUNRISE: _____ SUNSET: _____

ELEMENTS
WIND DIRECTION: _____ SPEED: _____
CIRCLE ONE: SUNNY – PARTLY CLOUDY – CLOUDY – RAINING – STORMING

PREHUNT PREP
BAIT:_____ STAND/BLIND: _____
SCENT:_____ CALL USED: _____
DECOY: _____
RESULTS: _____
_____

ANIMAL ACTIVITY
SIGHTINGS (CIRCLE)
FEEDING – DROPPINGS – TRACKS – SCRAPES/RUBS
OTHER:_____
NUMBER OF ANIMALS SEEN / SEX: _____

HARVEST NOTES
WEAPON USED: _____ ANIMAL SIZE: _____

OTHER FIELD NOTES:_____
_____
_____
_____
_____

HUNTING JOURNAL AND LOG BOOK

GAME BEING PERSUED _____

DATE: _____   TIME: _____   TO: _____

WEATHER DETAILS
CURRENT TEMP: _____   HIGH/LOW: _____ / _____
MOON PHASE: _____   BAROMETER: _____
SUNRISE: _____   SUNSET: _____

ELEMENTS
WIND DIRECTION: _____   SPEED: _____
CIRCLE ONE: SUNNY - PARTLY CLOUDY - CLOUDY - RAINING - STORMING

PREHUNT PREP
BAIT: _____   STAND/BLIND: _____
SCENT: _____   CALL USED: _____
DECOY: _____
RESULTS: _____
_____

ANIMAL ACTIVITY
SIGHTINGS (CIRCLE)
FEEDING - DROPPINGS - TRACKS - SCRAPES/RUBS
OTHER: _____
NUMBER OF ANIMALS SEEN / SEX: _____

HARVEST NOTES
WEAPON USED: _____   ANIMAL SIZE: _____

OTHER FIELD NOTES: _____
_____
_____
_____
_____

HUNTING JOURNAL AND LOG BOOK

GAME BEING PERSUED _____

DATE: _____ TIME: _____ TO: _____

WEATHER DETAILS
CURRENT TEMP: _____ HIGH/LOW: _____/_____
MOON PHASE: _____ BAROMETER: _____
SUNRISE: _____ SUNSET: _____

ELEMENTS
WIND DIRECTION: _____ SPEED: _____
CIRCLE ONE: SUNNY - PARTLY CLOUDY - CLOUDY - RAINING - STORMING

PREHUNT PREP
BAIT: _____ STAND/BLIND: _____
SCENT: _____ CALL USED: _____
DECOY: _____
RESULTS: _____
_____

ANIMAL ACTIVITY
SIGHTINGS (CIRCLE)
FEEDING - DROPPINGS - TRACKS - SCRAPES/RUBS
OTHER: _____
NUMBER OF ANIMALS SEEN / SEX: _____

HARVEST NOTES
WEAPON USED: _____ ANIMAL SIZE: _____

OTHER FIELD NOTES: _____
_____
_____
_____
_____

HUNTING JOURNAL AND LOG BOOK

GAME BEING PERSUED _____

DATE: _____ TIME: _____ TO: _____

WEATHER DETAILS
CURRENT TEMP: _____ HIGH/LOW: _____ / _____
MOON PHASE: _____ BAROMETER: _____
SUNRISE: _____ SUNSET: _____

ELEMENTS
WIND DIRECTION: _____ SPEED: _____
CIRCLE ONE: SUNNY – PARTLY CLOUDY – CLOUDY – RAINING – STORMING

PREHUNT PREP
BAIT: _____ STAND/BLIND: _____
SCENT: _____ CALL USED: _____
DECOY: _____
RESULTS: _____
_____

ANIMAL ACTIVITY
SIGHTINGS (CIRCLE)
FEEDING – DROPPINGS – TRACKS – SCRAPES/RUBS
OTHER: _____
NUMBER OF ANIMALS SEEN / SEX: _____

HARVEST NOTES
WEAPON USED: _____ ANIMAL SIZE: _____

OTHER FIELD NOTES: _____
_____
_____
_____
_____

HUNTING JOURNAL AND LOG BOOK

GAME BEING PERSUED _____

DATE: _____ TIME: _____ TO: _____

WEATHER DETAILS
CURRENT TEMP: _____ HIGH/LOW: _____ / _____
MOON PHASE: _____ BAROMETER: _____
SUNRISE: _____ SUNSET: _____

ELEMENTS
WIND DIRECTION: _____ SPEED: _____

CIRCLE ONE: SUNNY - PARTLY CLOUDY - CLOUDY - RAINING - STORMING

PREHUNT PREP
BAIT: _____ STAND/BLIND: _____
SCENT: _____ CALL USED: _____
DECOY: _____
RESULTS: _____
_____

ANIMAL ACTIVITY
SIGHTINGS (CIRCLE)
FEEDING - DROPPINGS - TRACKS - SCRAPES/RUBS
OTHER: _____
NUMBER OF ANIMALS SEEN / SEX: _____

HARVEST NOTES
WEAPON USED: _____ ANIMAL SIZE: _____

OTHER FIELD NOTES: _____
_____
_____
_____
_____

HUNTING JOURNAL AND LOG BOOK

GAME BEING PERSUED _____

DATE: _____   TIME: _____   TO: _____

WEATHER DETAILS
CURRENT TEMP: _____   HIGH/LOW: _____ / _____
MOON PHASE: _____   BAROMETER: _____
SUNRISE: _____   SUNSET: _____

ELEMENTS
WIND DIRECTION: _____   SPEED: _____

CIRCLE ONE: SUNNY - PARTLY CLOUDY - CLOUDY - RAINING - STORMING

PREHUNT PREP
BAIT: _____   STAND/BLIND: _____
SCENT: _____   CALL USED: _____
DECOY: _____
RESULTS: _____
_____

ANIMAL ACTIVITY
SIGHTINGS (CIRCLE)
FEEDING - DROPPINGS - TRACKS - SCRAPES/RUBS
OTHER: _____
NUMBER OF ANIMALS SEEN / SEX: _____

HARVEST NOTES
WEAPON USED: _____   ANIMAL SIZE: _____

OTHER FIELD NOTES: _____
_____
_____
_____
_____

HUNTING JOURNAL AND LOG BOOK

GAME BEING PERSUED _____

DATE: _____ TIME: _____ TO: _____

WEATHER DETAILS
CURRENT TEMP: _____ HIGH/LOW: _____ / _____
MOON PHASE: _____ BAROMETER: _____
SUNRISE: _____ SUNSET: _____

ELEMENTS
WIND DIRECTION: _____ SPEED: _____
CIRCLE ONE: SUNNY - PARTLY CLOUDY - CLOUDY - RAINING - STORMING

PREHUNT PREP
BAIT: _____ STAND/BLIND: _____
SCENT: _____ CALL USED: _____
DECOY: _____
RESULTS: _____
_____

ANIMAL ACTIVITY
SIGHTINGS (CIRCLE)
FEEDING - DROPPINGS - TRACKS - SCRAPES/RUBS
OTHER: _____
NUMBER OF ANIMALS SEEN / SEX: _____

HARVEST NOTES
WEAPON USED: _____ ANIMAL SIZE: _____

OTHER FIELD NOTES: _____
_____
_____
_____
_____

HUNTING JOURNAL AND LOG BOOK

GAME BEING PERSUED _____

DATE: _____ TIME: _____ TO: _____

WEATHER DETAILS
CURRENT TEMP: _____ HIGH/LOW: _____ / _____
MOON PHASE: _____ BAROMETER: _____
SUNRISE: _____ SUNSET: _____

ELEMENTS
WIND DIRECTION: _____ SPEED: _____
CIRCLE ONE: SUNNY – PARTLY CLOUDY – CLOUDY – RAINING – STORMING

PREHUNT PREP
BAIT: _____ STAND/BLIND: _____
SCENT: _____ CALL USED: _____
DECOY: _____
RESULTS: _____
_____

ANIMAL ACTIVITY
SIGHTINGS (CIRCLE)
FEEDING – DROPPINGS – TRACKS – SCRAPES/RUBS
OTHER: _____
NUMBER OF ANIMALS SEEN / SEX: _____

HARVEST NOTES
WEAPON USED: _____ ANIMAL SIZE: _____

OTHER FIELD NOTES: _____
_____
_____
_____
_____

HUNTING JOURNAL AND LOG BOOK

GAME BEING PERSUED _____

DATE: _____ TIME: _____ TO: _____

WEATHER DETAILS
CURRENT TEMP: _____ HIGH/LOW: _____ / _____
MOON PHASE: _____ BAROMETER: _____
SUNRISE: _____ SUNSET: _____

ELEMENTS
WIND DIRECTION: _____ SPEED: _____
CIRCLE ONE: SUNNY - PARTLY CLOUDY - CLOUDY - RAINING - STORMING

PREHUNT PREP
BAIT: _____ STAND/BLIND: _____
SCENT: _____ CALL USED: _____
DECOY: _____
RESULTS: _____
_____

ANIMAL ACTIVITY
SIGHTINGS (CIRCLE)
FEEDING - DROPPINGS - TRACKS - SCRAPES/RUBS
OTHER: _____
NUMBER OF ANIMALS SEEN / SEX: _____

HARVEST NOTES
WEAPON USED: _____ ANIMAL SIZE: _____

OTHER FIELD NOTES: _____
_____
_____
_____
_____

HUNTING JOURNAL AND LOG BOOK

GAME BEING PERSUED _____

DATE: _____ TIME: _____ TO: _____

WEATHER DETAILS
CURRENT TEMP: _____ HIGH/LOW: _____ / _____
MOON PHASE: _____ BAROMETER: _____
SUNRISE: _____ SUNSET: _____

ELEMENTS
WIND DIRECTION: _____ SPEED: _____
CIRCLE ONE: SUNNY - PARTLY CLOUDY - CLOUDY - RAINING - STORMING

PREHUNT PREP
BAIT: _____ STAND/BLIND: _____
SCENT: _____ CALL USED: _____
DECOY: _____
RESULTS: _____
_____

ANIMAL ACTIVITY
SIGHTINGS (CIRCLE)
FEEDING - DROPPINGS - TRACKS - SCRAPES/RUBS
OTHER: _____
NUMBER OF ANIMALS SEEN / SEX: _____

HARVEST NOTES
WEAPON USED: _____ ANIMAL SIZE: _____

OTHER FIELD NOTES: _____
_____
_____
_____
_____

HUNTING JOURNAL AND LOG BOOK

GAME BEING PERSUED _____

DATE: _____ TIME: _____ TO: _____

WEATHER DETAILS
CURRENT TEMP: _____ HIGH/LOW: _____ / _____
MOON PHASE: _____ BAROMETER: _____
SUNRISE: _____ SUNSET: _____

ELEMENTS
WIND DIRECTION: _____ SPEED: _____
CIRCLE ONE: SUNNY – PARTLY CLOUDY – CLOUDY – RAINING – STORMING

PREHUNT PREP
BAIT: _____ STAND/BLIND: _____
SCENT: _____ CALL USED: _____
DECOY: _____
RESULTS: _____
_____

ANIMAL ACTIVITY
SIGHTINGS (CIRCLE)
FEEDING – DROPPINGS – TRACKS – SCRAPES/RUBS
OTHER: _____
NUMBER OF ANIMALS SEEN / SEX: _____

HARVEST NOTES
WEAPON USED: _____ ANIMAL SIZE: _____

OTHER FIELD NOTES: _____
_____
_____
_____
_____

HUNTING JOURNAL AND LOG BOOK

GAME BEING PERSUED _____

DATE: _____ TIME: _____ TO: _____

WEATHER DETAILS
CURRENT TEMP: _____ HIGH/LOW: _____ / _____
MOON PHASE: _____ BAROMETER: _____
SUNRISE: _____ SUNSET: _____

ELEMENTS
WIND DIRECTION: _____ SPEED: _____
CIRCLE ONE: SUNNY – PARTLY CLOUDY – CLOUDY – RAINING – STORMING

PREHUNT PREP
BAIT: _____ STAND/BLIND: _____
SCENT: _____ CALL USED: _____
DECOY: _____
RESULTS: _____
_____

ANIMAL ACTIVITY
SIGHTINGS (CIRCLE)
FEEDING – DROPPINGS – TRACKS – SCRAPES/RUBS
OTHER: _____
NUMBER OF ANIMALS SEEN / SEX: _____

HARVEST NOTES
WEAPON USED: _____ ANIMAL SIZE: _____

OTHER FIELD NOTES: _____
_____
_____
_____
_____

HUNTING JOURNAL AND LOG BOOK

GAME BEING PERSUED _____

DATE: _____ TIME: _____ TO: _____

WEATHER DETAILS
CURRENT TEMP: _____ HIGH/LOW: _____ / _____
MOON PHASE: _____ BAROMETER: _____
SUNRISE: _____ SUNSET: _____

ELEMENTS
WIND DIRECTION: _____ SPEED: _____
CIRCLE ONE: SUNNY - PARTLY CLOUDY - CLOUDY - RAINING - STORMING

PREHUNT PREP
BAIT: _____ STAND/BLIND: _____
SCENT: _____ CALL USED: _____
DECOY: _____
RESULTS: _____
_____

ANIMAL ACTIVITY
SIGHTINGS (CIRCLE)
FEEDING - DROPPINGS - TRACKS - SCRAPES/RUBS
OTHER: _____
NUMBER OF ANIMALS SEEN / SEX: _____

HARVEST NOTES
WEAPON USED: _____ ANIMAL SIZE: _____

OTHER FIELD NOTES: _____
_____
_____
_____
_____

HUNTING JOURNAL AND LOG BOOK

GAME BEING PERSUED _____

DATE: _____ TIME: _____ TO: _____

WEATHER DETAILS
CURRENT TEMP: _____ HIGH/LOW: _____ / _____
MOON PHASE: _____ BAROMETER: _____
SUNRISE: _____ SUNSET: _____

ELEMENTS
WIND DIRECTION: _____ SPEED: _____
CIRCLE ONE: SUNNY – PARTLY CLOUDY – CLOUDY – RAINING – STORMING

PREHUNT PREP
BAIT: _____ STAND/BLIND: _____
SCENT: _____ CALL USED: _____
DECOY: _____
RESULTS: _____
_____

ANIMAL ACTIVITY
SIGHTINGS (CIRCLE)
FEEDING – DROPPINGS – TRACKS – SCRAPES/RUBS
OTHER: _____
NUMBER OF ANIMALS SEEN / SEX: _____

HARVEST NOTES
WEAPON USED: _____ ANIMAL SIZE: _____

OTHER FIELD NOTES: _____
_____
_____
_____
_____

HUNTING JOURNAL AND LOG BOOK

GAME BEING PERSUED _____

DATE: _____ TIME: _____ TO: _____

WEATHER DETAILS
CURRENT TEMP: _____ HIGH/LOW:_____ / _____
MOON PHASE: _____ BAROMETER:_____
SUNRISE: _____ SUNSET: _____

ELEMENTS
WIND DIRECTION:_____ SPEED:_____

CIRCLE ONE: SUNNY - PARTLY CLOUDY - CLOUDY - RAINING - STORMING

PREHUNT PREP
BAIT:_____ STAND/BLIND: _____
SCENT:_____ CALL USED: _____
DECOY:_____
RESULTS: _____
_____

ANIMAL ACTIVITY
SIGHTINGS (CIRCLE)
FEEDING - DROPPINGS - TRACKS - SCRAPES/RUBS
OTHER:_____
NUMBER OF ANIMALS SEEN / SEX: _____

HARVEST NOTES
WEAPON USED: _____ ANIMAL SIZE: _____

OTHER FIELD NOTES: _____
_____
_____
_____
_____

HUNTING JOURNAL AND LOG BOOK

GAME BEING PERSUED _____

DATE: _____ TIME: _____ TO: _____

WEATHER DETAILS
CURRENT TEMP: _____ HIGH/LOW: _____ / _____
MOON PHASE: _____ BAROMETER: _____
SUNRISE: _____ SUNSET: _____

ELEMENTS
WIND DIRECTION: _____ SPEED: _____
CIRCLE ONE: SUNNY - PARTLY CLOUDY - CLOUDY - RAINING - STORMING

PREHUNT PREP
BAIT: _____ STAND/BLIND: _____
SCENT: _____ CALL USED: _____
DECOY: _____
RESULTS: _____
_____

ANIMAL ACTIVITY
SIGHTINGS (CIRCLE)
FEEDING - DROPPINGS - TRACKS - SCRAPES/RUBS
OTHER: _____
NUMBER OF ANIMALS SEEN / SEX: _____

HARVEST NOTES
WEAPON USED: _____ ANIMAL SIZE: _____

OTHER FIELD NOTES: _____
_____
_____
_____
_____

HUNTING JOURNAL AND LOG BOOK

GAME BEING PERSUED _____

DATE: _____ TIME: _____ TO: _____

WEATHER DETAILS
CURRENT TEMP: _____ HIGH/LOW: _____ / _____
MOON PHASE: _____ BAROMETER: _____
SUNRISE: _____ SUNSET: _____

ELEMENTS
WIND DIRECTION: _____ SPEED: _____
CIRCLE ONE: SUNNY – PARTLY CLOUDY – CLOUDY – RAINING – STORMING

PREHUNT PREP
BAIT: _____ STAND/BLIND: _____
SCENT: _____ CALL USED: _____
DECOY: _____
RESULTS: _____
_____

ANIMAL ACTIVITY
SIGHTINGS (CIRCLE)
FEEDING – DROPPINGS – TRACKS – SCRAPES/RUBS
OTHER: _____
NUMBER OF ANIMALS SEEN / SEX: _____

HARVEST NOTES
WEAPON USED: _____ ANIMAL SIZE: _____

OTHER FIELD NOTES: _____
_____
_____
_____
_____

HUNTING JOURNAL AND LOG BOOK

GAME BEING PERSUED _____

DATE: _____ TIME: _____ TO: _____

WEATHER DETAILS
CURRENT TEMP: _____ HIGH/LOW: _____/_____
MOON PHASE: _____ BAROMETER: _____
SUNRISE: _____ SUNSET: _____

ELEMENTS
WIND DIRECTION: _____ SPEED: _____
CIRCLE ONE: SUNNY - PARTLY CLOUDY - CLOUDY - RAINING - STORMING

PREHUNT PREP
BAIT: _____ STAND/BLIND: _____
SCENT: _____ CALL USED: _____
DECOY: _____
RESULTS: _____
_____

ANIMAL ACTIVITY
SIGHTINGS (CIRCLE)
FEEDING - DROPPINGS - TRACKS - SCRAPES/RUBS
OTHER: _____
NUMBER OF ANIMALS SEEN / SEX: _____

HARVEST NOTES
WEAPON USED: _____ ANIMAL SIZE: _____

OTHER FIELD NOTES: _____
_____
_____
_____
_____

HUNTING JOURNAL AND LOG BOOK

GAME BEING PERSUED _____

DATE: _____   TIME: _____   TO: _____

WEATHER DETAILS
CURRENT TEMP: _____   HIGH/LOW: _____ / _____
MOON PHASE: _____   BAROMETER: _____
SUNRISE: _____   SUNSET: _____

ELEMENTS
WIND DIRECTION: _____   SPEED: _____
CIRCLE ONE: SUNNY – PARTLY CLOUDY – CLOUDY – RAINING – STORMING

PREHUNT PREP
BAIT: _____   STAND/BLIND: _____
SCENT: _____   CALL USED: _____
DECOY: _____
RESULTS: _____
_____

ANIMAL ACTIVITY
SIGHTINGS (CIRCLE)
FEEDING – DROPPINGS – TRACKS – SCRAPES/RUBS
OTHER: _____
NUMBER OF ANIMALS SEEN / SEX: _____

HARVEST NOTES
WEAPON USED: _____   ANIMAL SIZE: _____

OTHER FIELD NOTES: _____
_____
_____
_____
_____

HUNTING JOURNAL AND LOG BOOK

GAME BEING PERSUED _____

DATE: _____ TIME: _____ TO: _____

WEATHER DETAILS
CURRENT TEMP: _____ HIGH/LOW: _____ / _____
MOON PHASE: _____ BAROMETER: _____
SUNRISE: _____ SUNSET: _____

ELEMENTS
WIND DIRECTION: _____ SPEED: _____
CIRCLE ONE: SUNNY – PARTLY CLOUDY – CLOUDY – RAINING – STORMING

PREHUNT PREP
BAIT: _____ STAND/BLIND: _____
SCENT: _____ CALL USED: _____
DECOY: _____
RESULTS: _____
_____

ANIMAL ACTIVITY
SIGHTINGS (CIRCLE)
FEEDING – DROPPINGS – TRACKS – SCRAPES/RUBS
OTHER: _____
NUMBER OF ANIMALS SEEN / SEX: _____

HARVEST NOTES
WEAPON USED: _____ ANIMAL SIZE: _____

OTHER FIELD NOTES: _____
_____
_____
_____
_____

HUNTING JOURNAL AND LOG BOOK

GAME BEING PERSUED _____

DATE: _____   TIME: _____   TO: _____

WEATHER DETAILS
CURRENT TEMP: _____   HIGH/LOW:_____/_____
MOON PHASE: _____   BAROMETER:_____
SUNRISE: _____   SUNSET:_____

ELEMENTS
WIND DIRECTION:_____   SPEED:_____

CIRCLE ONE: SUNNY - PARTLY CLOUDY - CLOUDY - RAINING - STORMING

PREHUNT PREP
BAIT:_____   STAND/BLIND: _____
SCENT:_____   CALL USED: _____
DECOY:_____
RESULTS: _____
_____

ANIMAL ACTIVITY
SIGHTINGS (CIRCLE)
FEEDING - DROPPINGS - TRACKS - SCRAPES/RUBS
OTHER: _____
NUMBER OF ANIMALS SEEN / SEX: _____

HARVEST NOTES
WEAPON USED: _____   ANIMAL SIZE: _____

OTHER FIELD NOTES: _____
_____
_____
_____
_____

HUNTING JOURNAL AND LOG BOOK

GAME BEING PERSUED _____

DATE: _____ TIME: _____ TO: _____

WEATHER DETAILS
CURRENT TEMP: _____ HIGH/LOW: _____ / _____
MOON PHASE: _____ BAROMETER: _____
SUNRISE: _____ SUNSET: _____

ELEMENTS
WIND DIRECTION: _____ SPEED: _____
CIRCLE ONE: SUNNY - PARTLY CLOUDY - CLOUDY - RAINING - STORMING

PREHUNT PREP
BAIT: _____ STAND/BLIND: _____
SCENT: _____ CALL USED: _____
DECOY: _____
RESULTS: _____
_____

ANIMAL ACTIVITY
SIGHTINGS (CIRCLE)
FEEDING - DROPPINGS - TRACKS - SCRAPES/RUBS
OTHER: _____
NUMBER OF ANIMALS SEEN / SEX: _____

HARVEST NOTES
WEAPON USED: _____ ANIMAL SIZE: _____

OTHER FIELD NOTES: _____
_____
_____
_____
_____

HUNTING JOURNAL AND LOG BOOK

GAME BEING PERSUED _____

DATE: _____ TIME: _____ TO: _____

WEATHER DETAILS
CURRENT TEMP: _____ HIGH/LOW: _____ / _____
MOON PHASE: _____ BAROMETER: _____
SUNRISE: _____ SUNSET: _____

ELEMENTS
WIND DIRECTION: _____ SPEED: _____
CIRCLE ONE: SUNNY – PARTLY CLOUDY – CLOUDY – RAINING – STORMING

PREHUNT PREP
BAIT: _____ STAND/BLIND: _____
SCENT: _____ CALL USED: _____
DECOY: _____
RESULTS: _____
_____

ANIMAL ACTIVITY
SIGHTINGS (CIRCLE)
FEEDING – DROPPINGS – TRACKS – SCRAPES/RUBS
OTHER: _____
NUMBER OF ANIMALS SEEN / SEX: _____

HARVEST NOTES
WEAPON USED: _____ ANIMAL SIZE: _____

OTHER FIELD NOTES: _____
_____
_____
_____
_____

HUNTING JOURNAL AND LOG BOOK

GAME BEING PERSUED _____

DATE: _____   TIME: _____   TO: _____

WEATHER DETAILS
CURRENT TEMP: _____   HIGH/LOW: _____ / _____
MOON PHASE: _____   BAROMETER: _____
SUNRISE: _____   SUNSET: _____

ELEMENTS
WIND DIRECTION: _____   SPEED: _____

CIRCLE ONE: SUNNY – PARTLY CLOUDY – CLOUDY – RAINING – STORMING

PREHUNT PREP
BAIT: _____   STAND/BLIND: _____
SCENT: _____   CALL USED: _____
DECOY: _____
RESULTS: _____
_____

ANIMAL ACTIVITY
SIGHTINGS (CIRCLE)
FEEDING – DROPPINGS – TRACKS – SCRAPES/RUBS
OTHER: _____
NUMBER OF ANIMALS SEEN / SEX: _____

HARVEST NOTES
WEAPON USED: _____   ANIMAL SIZE: _____

OTHER FIELD NOTES: _____
_____
_____
_____
_____

HUNTING JOURNAL AND LOG BOOK

GAME BEING PERSUED _____

DATE: _____   TIME: _____   TO: _____

WEATHER DETAILS
CURRENT TEMP: _____   HIGH/LOW: _____ / _____
MOON PHASE: _____   BAROMETER: _____
SUNRISE: _____   SUNSET: _____

ELEMENTS
WIND DIRECTION: _____   SPEED: _____

CIRCLE ONE: SUNNY – PARTLY CLOUDY – CLOUDY – RAINING – STORMING

PREHUNT PREP
BAIT: _____   STAND/BLIND: _____
SCENT: _____   CALL USED: _____
DECOY: _____
RESULTS: _____
_____

ANIMAL ACTIVITY
SIGHTINGS (CIRCLE)
FEEDING – DROPPINGS – TRACKS – SCRAPES/RUBS
OTHER: _____
NUMBER OF ANIMALS SEEN / SEX: _____

HARVEST NOTES
WEAPON USED: _____   ANIMAL SIZE: _____

OTHER FIELD NOTES: _____
_____
_____
_____
_____

HUNTING JOURNAL AND LOG BOOK

GAME BEING PERSUED _____

DATE: _____ TIME: _____ TO: _____

WEATHER DETAILS
CURRENT TEMP: _____ HIGH/LOW: _____ / _____
MOON PHASE: _____ BAROMETER: _____
SUNRISE: _____ SUNSET: _____

ELEMENTS
WIND DIRECTION: _____ SPEED: _____
CIRCLE ONE: SUNNY – PARTLY CLOUDY – CLOUDY – RAINING – STORMING

PREHUNT PREP
BAIT: _____ STAND/BLIND: _____
SCENT: _____ CALL USED: _____
DECOY: _____
RESULTS: _____
_____

ANIMAL ACTIVITY
SIGHTINGS (CIRCLE)
FEEDING – DROPPINGS – TRACKS – SCRAPES/RUBS
OTHER: _____
NUMBER OF ANIMALS SEEN / SEX: _____

HARVEST NOTES
WEAPON USED: _____ ANIMAL SIZE: _____

OTHER FIELD NOTES: _____
_____
_____
_____
_____

HUNTING JOURNAL AND LOG BOOK

GAME BEING PERSUED _____

DATE: _____ TIME: _____ TO: _____

WEATHER DETAILS
CURRENT TEMP: _____ HIGH/LOW: _____ / _____
MOON PHASE: _____ BAROMETER: _____
SUNRISE: _____ SUNSET: _____

ELEMENTS
WIND DIRECTION: _____ SPEED: _____
CIRCLE ONE: SUNNY - PARTLY CLOUDY - CLOUDY - RAINING - STORMING

PREHUNT PREP
BAIT: _____ STAND/BLIND: _____
SCENT: _____ CALL USED: _____
DECOY: _____
RESULTS: _____
_____

ANIMAL ACTIVITY
SIGHTINGS (CIRCLE)
FEEDING - DROPPINGS - TRACKS - SCRAPES/RUBS
OTHER: _____
NUMBER OF ANIMALS SEEN / SEX: _____

HARVEST NOTES
WEAPON USED: _____ ANIMAL SIZE: _____

OTHER FIELD NOTES: _____
_____
_____
_____
_____

HUNTING JOURNAL AND LOG BOOK

GAME BEING PERSUED _____

DATE: _____ TIME: _____ TO: _____

WEATHER DETAILS
CURRENT TEMP: _____ HIGH/LOW: _____ / _____
MOON PHASE: _____ BAROMETER: _____
SUNRISE: _____ SUNSET: _____

ELEMENTS
WIND DIRECTION: _____ SPEED: _____
CIRCLE ONE: SUNNY - PARTLY CLOUDY - CLOUDY - RAINING - STORMING

PREHUNT PREP
BAIT: _____ STAND/BLIND: _____
SCENT: _____ CALL USED: _____
DECOY: _____
RESULTS: _____
_____

ANIMAL ACTIVITY
SIGHTINGS (CIRCLE)
FEEDING - DROPPINGS - TRACKS - SCRAPES/RUBS
OTHER: _____
NUMBER OF ANIMALS SEEN / SEX: _____

HARVEST NOTES
WEAPON USED: _____ ANIMAL SIZE: _____

OTHER FIELD NOTES: _____
_____
_____
_____
_____

HUNTING JOURNAL AND LOG BOOK

GAME BEING PERSUED _____

DATE: _____ TIME: _____ TO: _____

WEATHER DETAILS
CURRENT TEMP: _____ HIGH/LOW: _____ / _____
MOON PHASE: _____ BAROMETER: _____
SUNRISE: _____ SUNSET: _____

ELEMENTS
WIND DIRECTION: _____ SPEED: _____
CIRCLE ONE: SUNNY – PARTLY CLOUDY – CLOUDY – RAINING – STORMING

PREHUNT PREP
BAIT: _____ STAND/BLIND: _____
SCENT: _____ CALL USED: _____
DECOY: _____
RESULTS: _____
_____

ANIMAL ACTIVITY
SIGHTINGS (CIRCLE)
FEEDING – DROPPINGS – TRACKS – SCRAPES/RUBS
OTHER: _____
NUMBER OF ANIMALS SEEN / SEX: _____

HARVEST NOTES
WEAPON USED: _____ ANIMAL SIZE: _____

OTHER FIELD NOTES: _____
_____
_____
_____
_____

HUNTING JOURNAL AND LOG BOOK

GAME BEING PERSUED _____

DATE: _____ TIME: _____ TO: _____

WEATHER DETAILS
CURRENT TEMP: _____ HIGH/LOW: _____ / _____
MOON PHASE: _____ BAROMETER: _____
SUNRISE: _____ SUNSET: _____

ELEMENTS
WIND DIRECTION: _____ SPEED: _____
CIRCLE ONE: SUNNY - PARTLY CLOUDY - CLOUDY - RAINING - STORMING

PREHUNT PREP
BAIT: _____ STAND/BLIND: _____
SCENT: _____ CALL USED: _____
DECOY: _____
RESULTS: _____
_____

ANIMAL ACTIVITY
SIGHTINGS (CIRCLE)
FEEDING - DROPPINGS - TRACKS - SCRAPES/RUBS
OTHER: _____
NUMBER OF ANIMALS SEEN / SEX: _____

HARVEST NOTES
WEAPON USED: _____ ANIMAL SIZE: _____

OTHER FIELD NOTES: _____
_____
_____
_____
_____

HUNTING JOURNAL AND LOG BOOK

GAME BEING PERSUED _____

DATE: _____ TIME: _____ TO: _____

WEATHER DETAILS
CURRENT TEMP: _____ HIGH/LOW: _____ / _____
MOON PHASE: _____ BAROMETER: _____
SUNRISE: _____ SUNSET: _____

ELEMENTS
WIND DIRECTION: _____ SPEED: _____
CIRCLE ONE: SUNNY - PARTLY CLOUDY - CLOUDY - RAINING - STORMING

PREHUNT PREP
BAIT: _____ STAND/BLIND: _____
SCENT: _____ CALL USED: _____
DECOY: _____
RESULTS: _____
_____

ANIMAL ACTIVITY
SIGHTINGS (CIRCLE)
FEEDING - DROPPINGS - TRACKS - SCRAPES/RUBS
OTHER: _____
NUMBER OF ANIMALS SEEN / SEX: _____

HARVEST NOTES
WEAPON USED: _____ ANIMAL SIZE: _____

OTHER FIELD NOTES: _____
_____
_____
_____
_____

HUNTING JOURNAL AND LOG BOOK

GAME BEING PERSUED _____

DATE: _____ TIME: _____ TO: _____

WEATHER DETAILS
CURRENT TEMP: _____ HIGH/LOW: _____ / _____
MOON PHASE: _____ BAROMETER: _____
SUNRISE: _____ SUNSET: _____

ELEMENTS
WIND DIRECTION: _____ SPEED: _____
CIRCLE ONE: SUNNY – PARTLY CLOUDY – CLOUDY – RAINING – STORMING

PREHUNT PREP
BAIT: _____ STAND/BLIND: _____
SCENT: _____ CALL USED: _____
DECOY: _____
RESULTS: _____
_____

ANIMAL ACTIVITY
SIGHTINGS (CIRCLE)
FEEDING – DROPPINGS – TRACKS – SCRAPES/RUBS
OTHER: _____
NUMBER OF ANIMALS SEEN / SEX: _____

HARVEST NOTES
WEAPON USED: _____ ANIMAL SIZE: _____

OTHER FIELD NOTES: _____
_____
_____
_____
_____

HUNTING JOURNAL AND LOG BOOK

GAME BEING PERSUED _____

DATE: _____ TIME: _____ TO: _____

WEATHER DETAILS
CURRENT TEMP: _____ HIGH/LOW: _____ / _____
MOON PHASE: _____ BAROMETER: _____
SUNRISE: _____ SUNSET: _____

ELEMENTS
WIND DIRECTION: _____ SPEED: _____
CIRCLE ONE: SUNNY – PARTLY CLOUDY – CLOUDY – RAINING – STORMING

PREHUNT PREP
BAIT: _____ STAND/BLIND: _____
SCENT: _____ CALL USED: _____
DECOY: _____
RESULTS: _____
_____

ANIMAL ACTIVITY
SIGHTINGS (CIRCLE)
FEEDING – DROPPINGS – TRACKS – SCRAPES/RUBS
OTHER: _____
NUMBER OF ANIMALS SEEN / SEX: _____

HARVEST NOTES
WEAPON USED: _____ ANIMAL SIZE: _____

OTHER FIELD NOTES: _____
_____
_____
_____
_____

HUNTING JOURNAL AND LOG BOOK

GAME BEING PERSUED _____

DATE: _____ TIME: _____ TO: _____

WEATHER DETAILS
CURRENT TEMP: _____ HIGH/LOW: _____ / _____
MOON PHASE: _____ BAROMETER: _____
SUNRISE: _____ SUNSET: _____

ELEMENTS
WIND DIRECTION: _____ SPEED: _____
CIRCLE ONE: SUNNY - PARTLY CLOUDY - CLOUDY - RAINING - STORMING

PREHUNT PREP
BAIT: _____ STAND/BLIND: _____
SCENT: _____ CALL USED: _____
DECOY: _____
RESULTS: _____
_____

ANIMAL ACTIVITY
SIGHTINGS (CIRCLE)
FEEDING - DROPPINGS - TRACKS - SCRAPES/RUBS
OTHER: _____
NUMBER OF ANIMALS SEEN / SEX: _____

HARVEST NOTES
WEAPON USED: _____ ANIMAL SIZE: _____

OTHER FIELD NOTES: _____
_____
_____
_____
_____

HUNTING JOURNAL AND LOG BOOK

GAME BEING PERSUED _____

DATE: _____ TIME: _____ TO: _____

WEATHER DETAILS
CURRENT TEMP: _____ HIGH/LOW: _____ / _____
MOON PHASE: _____ BAROMETER: _____
SUNRISE: _____ SUNSET: _____

ELEMENTS
WIND DIRECTION: _____ SPEED: _____
CIRCLE ONE: SUNNY - PARTLY CLOUDY - CLOUDY - RAINING - STORMING

PREHUNT PREP
BAIT: _____ STAND/BLIND: _____
SCENT: _____ CALL USED: _____
DECOY: _____
RESULTS: _____
_____

ANIMAL ACTIVITY
SIGHTINGS (CIRCLE)
FEEDING - DROPPINGS - TRACKS - SCRAPES/RUBS
OTHER: _____
NUMBER OF ANIMALS SEEN / SEX: _____

HARVEST NOTES
WEAPON USED: _____ ANIMAL SIZE: _____

OTHER FIELD NOTES: _____
_____
_____
_____
_____

HUNTING JOURNAL AND LOG BOOK

GAME BEING PERSUED _____

DATE: _____ TIME: _____ TO: _____

WEATHER DETAILS
CURRENT TEMP: _____ HIGH/LOW: _____ / _____
MOON PHASE: _____ BAROMETER: _____
SUNRISE: _____ SUNSET: _____

ELEMENTS
WIND DIRECTION: _____ SPEED: _____
CIRCLE ONE: SUNNY – PARTLY CLOUDY – CLOUDY – RAINING – STORMING

PREHUNT PREP
BAIT: _____ STAND/BLIND: _____
SCENT: _____ CALL USED: _____
DECOY: _____
RESULTS: _____
_____

ANIMAL ACTIVITY
SIGHTINGS (CIRCLE)
FEEDING – DROPPINGS – TRACKS – SCRAPES/RUBS
OTHER: _____
NUMBER OF ANIMALS SEEN / SEX: _____

HARVEST NOTES
WEAPON USED: _____ ANIMAL SIZE: _____

OTHER FIELD NOTES: _____
_____
_____
_____
_____